The Old House Book of
Living Rooms
and Parlors

The Old House Book of
Living Rooms and Parlors

Lawrence Grow, General Editor
James H. Roper, Consultant

WARNER BOOKS

A Warner Communications Company

Designed by Carl Berkowitz

Warner Books, Inc.
75 Rockefeller Plaza
New York, N.Y. 10019

 A Warner Communications Company

Printed in the United States of America

First printing: October 1980

10 9 8 7 6 5 4 3 2 1

Library of Congress Cataloging in Publication Data

GROW, LAWRENCE.
    THE OLD HOUSE BOOK OF LIVING ROOMS AND PARLORS.

    1. LIVING ROOMS.   2. INTERIOR DECORATION.
I. ROPER, JAMES H. II. TITLE.
NK2117.L5G76   747.7'5   80-18235
ISBN 0-446-51215-X (hardcover)
ISBN 0-446-97552-4 (pbk. U.S.A.)
ISBN 0-446-97779-9 (Canada)

Contents

Preface

Those who make old houses their homes frequently lament the lack of useful printed material concerning period interior design. At one extreme are technical treatises invaluable to individuals undertaking significant restoration projects; at the other extreme are informal articles often devoted more to the application of colorful cosmetic touches than to the essential matters of design. *The Old House Book* series, of which *Living Rooms and Parlors* is the first volume, aims to provide the home decorator and restorer with fundamental information in an historical context. Information on how and in what manner families lived in the past—whether 75 or 250 years ago—is a prime requisite in such a volume. So, too, are examples of how the past is being interpreted today in homes throughout North America. *The Old House Book of Living Rooms and Parlors* presents such a blend of background information and present-day experience.

In bringing together widely diverse materials, both historical and contemporary, the assistance of the Historic American Buildings Survey, Washington, D.C. (now part of the National Architectural and Engineering Record) has been invaluable. Al Chambers and Carter Christianson of the HABS staff, and Mary Ison of the Prints

and Photographs Division of the Library of Congress have assisted in retrieving useful visual material. Equally enthusiastic and helpful have been those members of local, regional, and national historic preservation societies and consultants in the field who have tracked down fresh and imaginative approaches to period interior design across the country. This was often difficult as only houses which serve as private dwellings and which have not been widely publicized have been photographed and documented for this volume. For sharing their expertise, Gary Kray, Anne Baker, George Pearl, John Conron, and the Valenta family are especially thanked.

Introduction

"Things New and Old," from *The House Beautiful* (1881) by Clarence Cook. The mixing of antique and contemporary furnishings was strongly recommended by sophisticated writers on interior decoration in the late 1800s.

Adaptive reuse, or the recycling of old buildings for new uses, is now the key argument used by professional preservationists in the continuing battle to save something of the past. There is no longer much difficulty encountered in holding on to a truly historic house or even that which embodies the best of a distinct architectural style. The *average* old house, however, is probably neither historic nor stylistically important. It has stayed in place because someone loved it or, perhaps more realistically, because no one could afford to replace it. The classic candidate for adaptive reuse is a commercial building that has outlived its original function, but private homes can be and are adapted to new living purposes. To gut a whole building, preserving only a period façade, seems a particularly callous and wasteful exercise. On the other hand, turning the clock back in interior design need not be a static undertaking; preservation no longer means freezing time in place, and restoration does not call for the use of only candlelight and an outhouse. Some modernization is always essential. At the same time, however, a truly gracious old home must display its age, honestly and with dignity.

Original specifications for houses built in almost any period indicate that the space designated as the parlor or living room was to receive the best mantel, the most detailed moldings and other ornamentation, the finest flooring, the hardest wall finish of any room. The reason for this is fairly simple: because the parlor has been the room used traditionally for entertaining guests, it has had to be the "best" in virtually every respect. The need to present as good a picture to the outside world as possible has also resulted over the years in the continued redecoration of the room according to the dictates of fashion. Although a single living room or parlor may have been "done over" several times during its lifetime, the basic structural outlines of the space, however, were probably retained during remodeling—and these provide the basis for approaching the room's restoration.

The temptation to depend on cosmetic effects in restoration must be resisted. As the following chapters make clear, the use of matching papers and fabrics, reproduction lighting fixtures, and veneered paneling alone will not suffice to bring a room alive in a harmonious way if the basic proportions of the space are not respected. Providing a room with matching pieces of fur-

"My Lady's Chamber," as pictured in *The House Beautiful*, was always kept in a state of perfect order even if tea was for only one.

niture may also be less than satisfactory if these proportions are not honored. As Harold Peterson points out in his book *American Interiors,* the furniture shown in historic drawings, prints, paintings, and photographs "is often of widely varying ages and qualities, seldom of a single period, style or cost." There are, however, decorative schemes representative of various periods of interior design which, if carried out with craftsmanship and with quality materials, can allow for both a successful mix of objects and the feel of a particular stylistic period.

The ways in which a room has been heated, lighted, and structurally defined will have dictated its use and decoration over the years. A decision on whether to restore a room to its original state or one achieved at a later period of time should depend to a large extent on the overall architectural character of the house. Unless a building has been drastically altered—say from the Georgian Colonial form of the mid-1700s to the Second Empire mansard-roofed profile of the 1860s and '70s—it is best to return to the earlier state, at least to the point in time when the original style was most completely expressed. In restoring a New England salt-box begun in the late 17th century, for instance, it would be ridiculous to turn back to the time when it was only a one-room deep, two-room wide structure without a lean-to addition. Few of us are prepared to erect a four-poster in our living room, much less sleep there, as would have been the case in 17th-century America.

Utility—today's needs—will have a great deal to do with what restoration plan is agreed upon. Thousands of dollars can be spent in carefully channeling electric wires into stone walls; for only a few hundred, these can be hidden in proper cables in baseboards. And much can be done at a minimum expense if we can acquire the skills and the patience to perform such tasks ourselves, to take advantage of what professionals call "sweat equity." The eclectic nature of most American interiors of the past —the blending of at least two stylistically-defined periods within the same structure —is readily apparent in the documents of the past and should serve to remind us that in America a true period room is almost always a fiction, an artificial construct. A museum room should remain as a model, an ideal from which to work, but not as a pattern from which to copy slavishly.

Parlor, Price-Turner House, Lynchburg, Virginia, photo c. 1910. As late as the 20th century, this room included such early 19th-century furnishings as the Grecian scrolled armchair-rocker at right and the pole screen to the left of the fireplace. Wall-to-wall carpeting was also passé, and in this case had been laid many years earlier.

Living Room, Turlock, California, 1942. In homes from the 1920s on, the centerpiece of the living room was no longer the fireplace, but the radio console, here proudly decorated with a floral offering. Now, of course, it has been replaced by the television set. Just how important the fireplace has been as the focal point of interior decoration in old houses is discussed in the following chapter.

1.
The Living Room and Parlor: A History

Only in the 20th century have most people called the central and most public interior space in a house the "living room." Before the 1900s, all of the principal rooms on the first floor of a house, excluding the kitchen and a possible bedroom, were sometimes collectively termed the "living rooms." Although the term "living room" (in the singular) was included in the plans for very modest dwellings as early as the mid-19th century in American building guides, these homes were for families able to afford only one formal downstairs room. By the end of the 19th century, however, just about everyone except for the very rich was interested in trading in a "parlor" for a "living room." The rich preferred a "drawing room." Clarence Cook in his 1881 book, *The House Beautiful,* was in the vanguard:

I use the word "Living-Room" instead of "Parlor," because I am not intending to have anything to say about parlors. As these chapters are not written for rich people's reading, and as none but rich people can afford to have a room in their houses set apart for the pleasures of idleness, nothing would be gained by talking about such rooms. I should like to persuade a few young people who are just pushing their life-boat off shore to venture into deeper and more adventurous seas, that it will make their home a great deal more cheerful and home-like if they concentrate their leisure, in-door hours in one place, and do not attempt to keep up a room in which they themselves shall be strangers, and which will make a stranger of every friend who comes into it.

The specialized use of interior space had become terribly complicated by Cook's day, and the furnishing and etiquette of the front parlor quite constricting. Use of

Drawing room/ballroom, James Brice House, Annapolis, Maryland, 1766-73, Thomas Jennings, builder. The classic Georgian Colonial interior design is attributed to William Buckland and features molded plaster decoration and richly carved wood detail.

the term "living room" was thus seen as an improvement and was a reflection of a need to break away from Victorian convention.

Before this time many of our ancestors knew only of a parlor or sitting room, or of such earlier labels as "salon," "drawing room," "reception," "gathering room," "hall," or "keeping room." Just how the living room space was known at a particular

Parlor, Cady House, Sonoma, California, photograph c. 1885. Lavish house plants are nothing new in the American home. From the mid-19th century on, vines were used as wall festoons and to garland pictures; hanging baskets and potted plants commonly were arranged in a sunny alcove.

Front parlor, Alfred Chartz House, Carson City, Nevada, c. 1876. Some would call the typically overdecorated parlor cluttered; others find the piling up of ornament and object an utter delight.

time depended on several factors: the style, period, and geographic area in which the house was built and, in some cases, the social status of the owner. A prosperous family in the Boston area or in tidewater Virginia during the early 18th century may have lived in a house with a hall, an area specifically set aside as a family gathering place and for entertaining guests. The hall was quite distinct from the entry-way. In the rural New England of the same period, there might be only an all-purpose keeping room which served as a kitchen, dining room, communal living room, and perhaps even as a bedroom at night. Enlarged by the addition of new wings during the mid-1700s to early 1800s, such a farmhouse

would then have included a parlor. A double parlor—two adjoining rooms—might even have been provided for in the renovation; such an arrangement became traditional in middle-class homes built during the Victorian period. Traditional, too, was the use of one of the parlors as a library or dining room. As one writer has noted in a recent *New York Times* article on today's use of the living room, some families residing in Victorian houses still prefer to gather in the back "library," the living room or drawing room being much too formal a place in which to relax.

In speaking of the parlor or living room, we are then referring to a fairly formal area. This was its essential character except in the earliest years of pioneering. In the 17th century only necessity dictated its use as a bedroom, although the bed furnishings were sometimes of a rather elaborate sort: hangings and coverings thought worthy of public view. While in different periods of our own century the parlor or living room came to include such informal modern conveniences as a gramophone, radio console, or television set, people of the "better sort" rarely allowed such intrusions; these disturbers of polite decorum were banished to a "family" or "rumpus" room. Only in the late 20th century are we beginning to rethink the social conventions accepted without question earlier. It has become too expensive to include a separate formal living room in many new homes and apartments, and the movement back to a multi-purpose living space, not unlike that known in the early Colonial or frontier

periods, grows every year.

Standing at the symbolic and physical center of nearly every period living room has been the fireplace. Edith Wharton and Ogden Codman could not have been more explicit in their advice tendered in *The Decoration of Houses* (1902): "The fireplace must be the focus of every rational scheme of arrangement." A functional element in most homes until the end of the 19th century, the fireplace determined in large part how a room was used and its furniture arranged. For this reason, Wharton and Codman were particularly upset by one thoughtless architectural practice which had become commonplace in the 1800s: "Nothing is so dreary, so hopeless to deal with, as a room in which the fireplace occupies a narrow space between two doors, so that it is impossible to sit about the hearth." Bad as this situation might have

Front parlor, John Sydenham House, Newark, New Jersey, mid-18th century. The house was built when the surrounding area was primarily rural and was expanded several times in the early 19th century. The early residents were unlikely to have used oriental carpets on the floor or to have been quite as neat in their housekeeping as this modern photograph suggests.

Parlor, Graves House, Montgomery, Alabama, mid-19th century. The studied architectural symmetry of the early Victorian parlor, with its center table and imposing mantel, is expressed in this early photo from the Historic American Buildings Survey archives. The hanging Tiffany-style lamp is of a later date than the room itself.

Top: Parlor, Hopewell, Frederick County, Maryland, early 19th century. The hearth as the symbolic center of domstic life is epitomized in the parlor mantel which includes silhouette insets of the first owner and his wife. *Above:* Drawing room mantel and mirror overmantel, Mills-Stebbins Villa, Springfield, Massachusetts, 1849-51. Built in the Italian Villa style, the house is a more modest version of the type pictured on page 49; the use of an ornate overmantel mirror is very similar and typical of those found in mid-century homes.

been, homes *without* fireplaces, in their view, were totally without aesthetic salvation.

The attention first given to the fireplace and its attendant elements—the hearth, the surround, the mantel, the overmantel or chimney breast, and occasionally a bake oven—is clearly evident in the paneled room ends of both modest and elaborate English Colonial period homes. It is also obvious in the massive corner fireplaces of Dutch and Spanish Colonial interiors of the same time. Only gradually during the 18th and 19th centuries did the fireplace begin to shrink somewhat in importance as well as in size. Parlor stoves vented through the chimney flue were used from at least the late 1700s on to provide the heat thrown previously by an open fire. The stoves could be positioned either on the hearth or set within the opening itself. Fueled by wood, and later coal, they eventually were replaced by gas heaters. Today, of course, the parlor stove has returned, and many a fireplace closed up in the 1800s and re-opened again in recent years to restore it to the original state, is now being used with a 20th-century version of the radiant stove that once warmed our ancestors. It may go against our modern "Colonial" sensibility to insert such a device, but the parlor stove vented through the fireplace is by no means ahistorical. Those which can be removed during the warmer months are to be preferred today.

The placement of a fireplace is determined in a period home, of course, by the chimney. The typical chimney in a 17th or 18th-century New England or Middle Atlantic home was positioned either within the gable end or, in the case of the Georgian Colonial, in the symmetrical center of the building, and possibly at each end as well. Depending on the thickness of the walls, chimneys were likely to jut out into a room, a not unpleasant occurrence, but sometimes the space on each side was furred out to make one continuous wall surface. After 1720 the fireplace, whether built into an exterior or an interior wall, was increasingly provided with a mantel. In Southern homes, the chimney was often built outside the exterior wall, but the result — in the interior — was much the same since a mantel was still applied to the fireplace.

Central heating was gradually introduced in many upper-class homes from the early 1800s on, but, until at least the turn of the century, a majority of families made do with space heaters of various sorts that were placed in or just outside a fireplace and vented through a chimney flue. When hot water systems came into use in the mid-19th century, the radiator was introduced. Thought to be hopelessly antique in the 1940s and '50s, such devices have survived mainly in only those buildings where the cost of converting to the use of baseboards was prohibitive. Today, however, there is a renewed appreciation of a radiator's utility. It can concentrate heat in one area of a room rather than spreading it thinly throughout the space; individual units can be turned off without affecting the operation of others. Many of the early models were quite ornate, handsome affairs, and the proud owner of such objects might even have inserted one in the parlor fireplace — if such still existed.

A central source of heat meant, of course, that there was no real need for fireplaces, and some houses built after the mid-1800s — especially in the Northern states — dispensed with such traditional trappings altogether. Nonetheless, the custom of including a fireplace — at least in the living room or parlor — survived the ad-

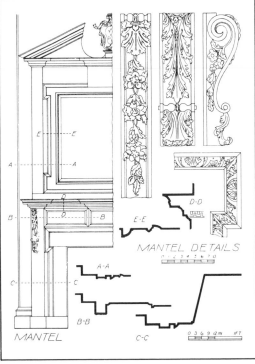

Top: Parlor mantel and overmantel mirror, Slater House, Connecticut, mid-19th century. *Above:* Mantel and overmantel details, drawing room, Powel House, Philadelphia, 1768. The very elaborate forms and combination of panels and molding used to define the Georgian Colonial fireplace in a formal room are carefully delineated in this measuring drawing.

vance of heating technology. Although basically ornamental, the fireplace remained the primary focus of attention in the room's composition. Towering oak mantels and mirrored overmantels dominate the space in many Queen Anne-style parlors of the 1880s. During the period of the Colonial Revival, from the 1890s through the 1920s, no living room or salon could be considered finished without an Adam-style mantel or an even fancier Georgian raised-panel chimney breast. There may have been no chimney behind it, no possible way to use the fireplace, but a formal downstairs room just didn't seem right without at least a mantel — regardless of the style of the house.

The furnishings and the very arrangement of furniture in such rooms were re-

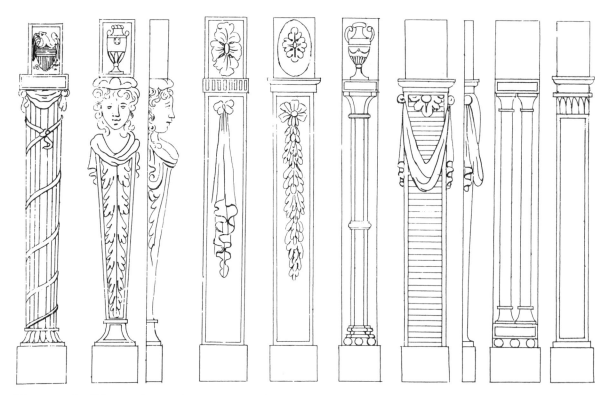

"Fragments for Chimney Pieces," Asher Benjamin, *The American Builder's Companion* (first edition, 1806). Decoration of the mantel became more detailed and neoclassical during the Federal period.

lated to the position of the fireplace, even after it had ceased to serve a functional purpose. The family hearth is such a strong symbol of domesticity in North America, of communal life, that it would seem at times that even the façade—the fake fireplace—found in many later 19th and early 20th-century homes was thought to radiate comfort to those surrounding it. Only in recent years has furniture been pulled away from the "fire," this central altar of the home, into freer standing groupings. As is clear from today's contemporary furnishings, one or more pieces of furniture have to be massive and low-slung to serve as an anchor for a space without the focal point of a fireplace. Now, increasingly, the fireplace is coming back into fashion, and the furniture is being pulled back around the hearth.

The other physical element which has determined the use of a living room or parlor and its furnishings is lighting. We often believe that a center fixture was always hung in an early period room, but the reverse is probably the case. Even modest chandeliers of wood or iron were not common during the Colonial period, and brass was rare; more likely to be found was a lantern which could be taken down and used elsewhere. Even more often there was no hanging fixture at all; rather, sconces were used against walls, and candlestands held holders of various kinds. Only during the early 19th century, after the introduction of whale oil and then kerosene, did the room become better illuminated. Following the Civil War, gas became common in cities

HOME COMFORT.

"Home Comfort," mid-19th-century advertisement. Thanks to the use of a parlor stove, Father could enjoy his evening reading of the newspaper; Mother upstairs kept at least her feet warm next to the ventilator which brought heat from the parlor. The bedchamber fireplace, not untypically, was kept closed.

Above: "Baltimore Stove, Base Burner," Wilson & Miller catalogue of the Keystone Slate Mantel and Slate Works, Philadelphia, 1874. The proprietors offered slate mantels to accommodate such a burner which they claimed could warm "the room in which it stands, and two or three rooms up stairs."

Top (Left): Parlor stove ("Ringgold Hot Blast"), Hinton Mansion, Petersburg, Virginia, photograph from 1935. Many homes in the South without central heating systems continued to use stoves vented through chimney flues well into the 20th century.

Left: "Hot-Air Stove," made by Learned & Thatcher, Albany, New York, and exhibited at the Great Exhibition of 1851, London. American manufacturers were as well known overseas for their stoves as for clocks and rocking chairs.

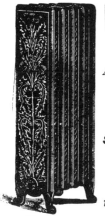
Advertisement, American Radiator Company, 1893.

and in rural towns where a family could afford the installation of an independent gasification system. An almost immediate result of the improvement in lighting was a freer arrangement of furniture. Chairs could be moved from the sides to the center, to surround what became standard in almost every Victorian parlor—a great and usually round table of oak, mahogany, or black walnut. If the fireplace was the center of family life during the 18th century, the center table, often draped with a fringed cloth upon which rested the family Bible, became a second focus of 19th century activity once the portability of improved lighting devices was perfected.

The table might have been part of a whole suite of parlor furniture in the Grecian or Empire, Gothic, Rococo Revival, or Renaissance Revival styles popular from the 1820s through the 1870s. The decoration of the room might change from decade to decade, its complexity increasing with the years, but the basic composition remained somewhat the same. Calvert Vaux's caustic description of such a room in 1864 could well apply to interiors of the 1850s or of the ten-year period after the Civil War:

A round table with a cloth on it, and a thin layer of books, in smart bindings, occupies the centre of the room, and furnishes accommodation enough for one rather small person to sit and write a note at. A gilt mirror finds a place between the windows. A sofa, by courtesy so-called, occupies irrevocably a well-defined space against the wall . . . There is also a row of black walnut chairs, with horse-hair seats, all ranged against the white wall. A console table, too, under the mirror, if I remember rightly, with a white marble top and thin gilt brackets. I think there is a piano. There is, certainly, a triangular stand for knicknacks, china, etc., and this, with some chimney ornaments, completes the furniture, which is all arranged according to stiff, immutable law.

Vaux compared the room he described to "a sort of quarantine in which to put each plague of a visitor that calls; and one almost expects to see the lady of the house walk in with a bottle of camphor in her hand, to prevent infection." The parlor of the late-Victorian period was a decidedly more comfortable room than that of the horsehair era of the mid-century, but no less formal an undertaking.

From the viewpoint of the 1980s, the Colonial Revival living room of 1900 seems similarly forbidding. Stripped of Victorian knickknackery and plush, it appears unfit for modern daily family use. The "best" downstairs room in most early 20th century homes—whether called a living room or parlor—was not any less formal than its predecessors. The center table had been removed, but the room still had to be arranged and kept in a state nearing perfection. The formality is even seen in the homey interiors of Mission Revival and Craftsman residences and, most markedly, in the architecturally-shaped living rooms of the Prairie School.

The living room, parlor, drawing room, salon, or hall of a period home has always been—in function—that space most carefully contrived and maintained. Its appointments and furnishings, however, have differed widely through the years. The use of particular kinds of architectural trimmings, fabrics, papers, paints and other finishes, and furniture can be traced over time. An understanding of various commonly-executed decorative schemes and of period styles—subjects to be explored in the following pages— is indispensable to the proper restoration and decoration of the space today.

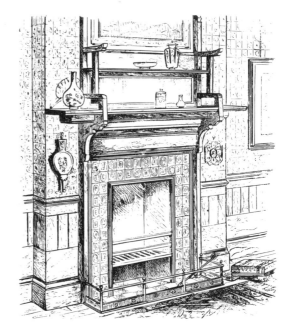

Top: "'T is home where'er the hearth is," proclaimed Clarence Cook in *The House Beautiful* (1881). No proper home was without one.

Above: A living room in what was termed the "Modern Mission" style, 1914. Most popular on the West Coast, Mission was nonetheless a look in vogue throughout the country.

Above: Center table, from *The Architecture of Country Houses* (1850) by A. J. Downing. The Victorian family gathered here as often as it did at the dining room table.

Top left: Gas chandelier, lacquered brass with glass globes, Cornelius & Baker, Philadelphia, exhibited at the Great Exhibition of 1851, London. The fixtures made by this firm were usually not quite so elaborate, but they were no less carefully made.

Left: Brass kerosene library lamp, with spring extension, as advertised in the 1902 Sears, Roebuck catalogue. Fixtures of this sort were used in rural areas well into the 20th century.

Top: Front parlor, Roseland (Bowen House), Woodstock, Connecticut, mid-19th century. The upholstered parlor set displays the carved and pierced motifs that were used in furnishings of every sort from the 1830s to the 1850s.

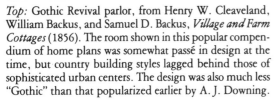

Top: Gothic Revival parlor, from Henry W. Cleaveland, William Backus, and Samuel D. Backus, *Village and Farm Cottages* (1856). The room shown in this popular compendium of home plans was somewhat passé in design at the time, but country building styles lagged behind those of sophisticated urban centers. The design was also much less "Gothic" than that popularized earlier by A. J. Downing.

Above: Fireplace and mantel, Mount Vernon, Indiana, 1880s, as adorned in 1937.

Above: Parlor, Warrenpoint (William Branson House), Chester County, Pennsylvania, 1756, as viewed in the 1890s. The mantel probably dates from the late 18th century and, by the time this photograph was taken, had been thoroughly adorned in a style which many late-Victorians considered appropriate for at least the summer months.

2.
The Essentials: Windows, Doors, Ceilings, and Floors

The space designated as the living room is often the best to be found in an old house. Well-lighted and airy, it is likely to have been chosen because it presented a cheerful appearance. If there was a choice in the matter in later years, as two Victorian experts declared in 1879, "select the brightest and most comfortable apartment in the house for the general room [the living room], for what are strangers and mere casual visitors compared with your own loved band?" It was good advice then and today. By the late 1870s, there may have been no other room to designate as a "living room," the sitting room of former days having been sacrificed for a dining room or even a bedroom. In modestly-priced new houses of the time, the parlor/living room was the only principal interior space for general use.

Since it has been used as much for the entertainment of outsiders as for the family itself, the living room is usually a front room that can be entered directly from the main entrance or entry hall of the house. In urban town houses of the 19th century built in narrow lots, beginning with those designed in the Federal style, the good parlor is the first of several rooms which stretch toward the rear. It may be joined to a back parlor, dining room, or sitting room by means of sliding doors or merely a simple archway. By its adaptation to either one large room or to two smaller ones, the so-called "double parlor" of the 19th century allowed for a cleverly functional use of interior space, a function still appreciated by those living in such houses today.

The earliest of the rooms used in the 17th century for general purposes were not at all well lit, but, then, few rooms were, the windows in most being nothing more than narrow casements or crude openings. Window glass was rarely used until the 18th century. English double sash replaced the casement form beginning in the 1720s and was used in homes built in the then-fashionable Georgian Colonial style. Increasing prosperity made possible a more elaborate treatment of the "hall," or what was being termed for the first time a parlor or drawing room. The wall against which the fireplace stood was that which received special care in the form of vertical paneling in imitation of ornate plasterwork. The room end, as this paneled wall is called, may have existed previously in the form of simple board sheathing, but in the 18th century it was redesigned along classical lines with an elaborate cornice, panels, pilasters, and a dado or flat space rising from the baseboard for several feet. A mantel or shelf was affixed to the chimney breast when none existed before.

Other walls in the typical Georgian Colonial parlor may have been plastered

Top: Back parlor looking to front parlor, "Roseland" (The Bowen House), Woodstock, Connecticut, mid-19th century. The flow of interior space provided the family with alternatives for its everyday and formal use. *Above:* Front parlor, "Roseland." The alcove formed by the bay window is an architectural feature of the sort recommended by A. J. Downing and Calvert Vaux to lend visual and spatial interest to the American home.

or, more commonly, simply whitewashed, and in some parlors the cornice was continued from the room end around all the walls. A chair rail or molding defined the middle wall panel area from that of the lower dado. Windows and doors were given molded casings of varying complexity, and in the best of houses the principal openings were crowned with pediments or architraves. The fireplace itself was placed in as central a position as the chimney would allow so as to throw as much heat into the room as possible, and the hearth became, as we have already seen, the focus by

which to arrange the room's furnishings.

The regularity of the Colonial-style parlor recommended it to the rational sensibility of the period. There was little alteration of the basic scheme through the 1820s, although window openings, in particular, were made larger, sometimes extending to the floor itself, and ceilings were raised much higher. Octagonal and round rooms were extremely rare. These alterations, however, only emphasized the formal and perhaps unduly severe look of the room. By the 1830s, a reaction to the symmetrical severity of the Georgian, Federal, and Greek Revival styles was beginning to set in. The Gothic Revival, the first of the romantic revivals to influence American domestic architecture, had been underway in England since the 1790s and in its purer form had little direct effect on 19th-century American builders. Rather, there was a slow borrowing of particular forms and types of ornamentation that could be added to the simpler American structure. A. J. Downing acquainted the public with the new asymmetrical "picturesque" mode in his several successful books, most notably *Cottage Residences* (1842) and *The Architecture of Country Houses* (1850). The façades of most domestic dwellings did not take on the character of a Swiss cottage or Tudor country house, but rather the regular features of what was called at the time an "Italian" villa of the Renaissance period. Likely to be found in the parlor of such a dwelling was one irregular feature popularized during the Gothic Revival and especially recommended by Downing—the bay window. As one of his colleagues, Calvert Vaux wrote in 1857: "A bay window is a very desirable addition to such a room, as it breaks up the monotony of outline, and gives a free and open effect."

Free and open effects were increasingly used during the course of the Victorian period—leaded glass, transoms, and Queen Anne windows; bracketed recesses and ceilings; multi-shelved and fretted or carved overmantels. Some houses of the inexpensive sort were built without fireplaces, but the builders of those of a better quality seemed to lavish even more attention on mantels which projected well into the room. Not until the 1890s was there the beginning of a popular return to the symmetrical design of the Colonial period.

The basic structural outline of the American parlor, nevertheless, did not change dramatically during the Victorian period. The addition of bay windows al-

lowed for a slightly more irregular treatment of space; ceilings probably reached their greatest height—11 to 12 feet—early in the century. In new homes, beams were plastered over. Their display was generally not considered attractive until the emergence of the Elizabethan and Shingle styles in the late 1800s. Flooring was almost always pine throughout both the Colonial and Victorian periods, narrowing gradually in width over time. Oak came into favor after the 1870s, and parquet was then a luxury first indulged by the wealthy. The most dramatic effects in the parlor were not of a structural sort but were those applied in the form of ornaments, paints, papers, fabrics, and furniture.

Southeast parlor looking to northeast parlor, "Rattle and Snap" (The Polk-Granberry House), vicinity of Columbia, Tennessee, 1845. The 52-foot-long double parlor of this late Greek Revival house provided a gracious ambience for formal entertainment. The monumental Corinthian columns and the elaborate cornice are reminiscent of the forms prescribed earlier in the century for neoclassical interiors.

Inside window and sliding shutter, Bradford-Huntington House, Norwichtown, Connecticut, c. 1691. The 12-over-12 sash window was certainly a replacement for a casement; the structure was altered several times during the 18th century.

Parlor fireplace wall, William Pepperrell House, Kittery Point, Maine, 1682. The fully wainscoted treatment of the room, with raised panels set in bolection moldings, probably dates from 1720-23 when the house was first remodeled. It is interesting to compare this wall with the fireplace wall in Warrenpoint, Chester County, Pennsylvania, page 22, to which a mantel was later added.

Parlor room end, William Pepperrell House.

Music room/drawing room, "Oaklands," Gardiner, Maine, 1835-37, designed by Richard Upjohn. This room is one of a row of three opening into each other. The building's principal first-floor rooms display the Tudor embellishments in the woodwork which are a trademark of the Gothic Revival style.

Entryway to parlor from main hall, Alabama, mid-19th century, photograph dates from the 1930s. A country builder with a flare for the romantic added a crown and applied ornament to a simple casing or door frame; the same treatment was given to interior windows.

Parlor entry, Alabama, mid-19th century. A very grand parlor or drawing room might be entered through sliding doors, these being set off by a full classical cornice with Corinthian columns *in antis*.

Bay window designs included in *Atwood's Country and Suburban Houses* (1871) were recommended to relieve the regularity of the usual American rural interior.

Elevation of Square Bay.
Scale, ⅛ of an inch.

Elevation of Octagonal Bay.
Scale, ⅛ of an inch.

Bay window, front parlor, G.W.G. Ferris House, Carson City, Nevada, late-19th century. The use of windowed projections, in this case a square bay, continued well into the Colonial Revival period of the early 1900s. The interior arches were often set off by ornamental brackets. For a similar treatment in an earlier California house see page 46.

Left: Shuttered double-hung windows, Mass House, Oakland, California, 1897. The large amount of light filtered through modern sash windows was often lessened in the late-Victorian house by the use of stained glass insets and interior shutters which folded back into the window casings. *Below:* Interior details, from "House at Summit, N.J.," *Modern Architectural Designs and Details* (1881) by William T. Comstock. Windows with multiple panes or lights were also employed to add period romance and privacy to Queen Anne homes.

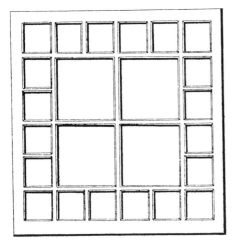

"Window Sash, Queen Anne Style," from *Modern Architectural Designs and Details.*

Southeast wall, drawing room, Villard House, New York City, McKim, Meade and White, architects, 1882-86. Opulent town houses in the Italian or French Renaissance taste preferred by Edith Wharton and Oliver Codman, Jr. (as expressed most fully in *The Decoration of Houses*) were and are rarities on the American scene. They and similarly detailed English Georgian homes reflect the late-19th-century revival of interest in the perfect symmetry and craftsmanship of an earlier aristocratic age.

Top: Parquet floor detail, Villard House.

Above: Fireplace inglenook, Frank Lloyd Wright Residence, Oak Park, Illinois, 1889. The massive Romanesque arched fireplace stands in almost direct stylistic opposition to the high-style European interpretations of the Beaux Arts school of the same period. This very early Wright interior follows and further defines in its composition and appointments the work of precursors H. H. Richardson and Louis Sullivan. For the similar use of a fireplace alcove or inglenook, see page 64.

3.
A Portfolio of Period Living Rooms and Parlors

Charm, architectural distinction, historical interest—each of these qualities in an older house appeals to those who wish to blend something of the past with their everyday life. Each building presents special challenges in this respect. The home restorer and decorator is likely to find that the historical record—what *was* done—may not be read easily. This is particularly true in the case of the average dwelling, one that is vernacular or somewhat nondescript in style, a building that might be best described as a "lady of a certain age." A majority of old houses in North America are of this type. Many carry the structural and decorative additions of at least several generations, changes made over the years which may or may not have added to the stylistic interest of the building and its interior spaces. Just how a home will be restored for new use will also be guided in large part by simple economics. As the interiors illustrated in the following pages suggest, however, it is not necessary to strip away all the additions of time and the patina of age in pursuit of a stylistically pure and original composition. Experience suggests that it would be wrong to do so. For each home there is an appropriate level of restoration, of adaptation which suits the needs of the present and respects the limits of the past.

This two-story Cape in the back country of Fairfield County, Connecticut, was first discovered and restored in the 1930s. The original dwelling, with enclosed gable-end chimney, dates from the 1750s. Probably extended to the left and certainly opened up to the right of the center beam, this rear sitting room was a great deal smaller and less open to natural light during the colonial period. The space as it exists today retains nonetheless the character of an 18th-century keeping room or kitchen, a place where a family of modest means would gather for various domestic activities before a living room or parlor was set aside for recreation and entertainment. The large stone fireplace includes a bake oven and the iron appliances needed for cooking. An oriental carpet was probably not used over the random-width pine floors before the 19th century; it makes sense in the 1980s.

An extremely handsome chimney breast or overmantel with raised paneling and a glass-front cupboard provide the center of attention in this room dating from the 1720s. The framing of the walls and ceilings is representative of the kind of structural work performed in rural areas of New England during the late 17th and early 18th centuries. The owner of the home, a preservation consultant, has used simple and comfortable furnishings which do not detract from the straightforward lines of the room.

From outward appearances, the house, located in Westport, Massachusetts, would seem to be typical of a symmetrical, New England dwelling with a center chimney. Nonetheless, this room, and others behind it, were added to a 1710 building with the chimney at the gable end. The new front room was clearly meant to serve as a parlor. It comprises the area immediately to the left of the front entrance, the original structure being situated to the right. The entire building was saved from destruction in the 1970s and was moved across the fields to a new site.

Seven difficult years were spent during the 1970s
reassembling a two-story half house from Swansea,
Massachusetts, on a new site in Westport, Massachusetts. The paneled room end was one of the ar-
chitecturally distinctive units to be put into place.
It rests now in the center of the house rather than
against an exterior wall, but none of its character
has been lost. The owners of the home are skilled
craftsmen and enjoy living in an interior which
proudly displays the artistry of many generations—a modern pottery lamp, a gracefully upholstered Empire-style sofa, a modern reproduction
iron candlestand, and an oriental carpet.

Above: Cool colors and rich woods bring out the simple lines of this mid-18th-century interior. A reproduction canvas floorcloth in a diamond pattern draws together the seating furniture in a logical, attractive grouping. Whether the beams or joists would have been exposed 200 years ago is conjectural. The windows were considerably enlarged in the mid-19th century. Residing in rural Monmouth County, New Jersey, the owners of this colonial clapboard home have searched far and wide for the work of pioneer New Jersey artisans. Their success is reflected in the corner cupboard, chest of drawers, and slant-front desk as well as in early 19th-century pastel portraits of members of the Hendrickson and Longstreet families by Micah Williams.

Opposite: In the 1860s this room and a new kitchen behind it were added to the Monmouth County house. Situated to the right of the entrance and center hall, the additional parlor was built without a fireplace although a chimney provided a flue opening for a stove. White pine floors were put down here rather than those of yellow pine used in the older section; the ceiling was paneled rather than left open or plastered.

Above: Restoring this 1803 Federal-style house in Newport, Rhode Island, has been a monumental task. Three apartments were carved out of its space in the 1900s, but fortunately the alterations had been made cheaply and without destroying the original floor plan. The right front parlor, one of two, has been given the most attention to date. Original paint colors have been documented and reproduced; the ornamented mantel was slowly stripped of layers of paint and the plaster decoration painstakingly uncovered. All the doors were originally grained, and the door at the right will be restored when time allows.

Opposite: The Ignacio de Roybal House, north of Santa Fe, New Mexico, is representative of dwellings built during the Spanish colonial period. A large hacienda, of which the present building was a part, was centered here in at least the mid-18th century. The *sala,* a reception and living room, lies just behind the portal. The windows, with their pedimented lintels, were changed somewhat in the mid-19th century and reflect the fashion favored by American settlers which has been termed by historians "the Territorial style." The furniture chosen for the room reflects the later decorative taste, and is in keeping with the weighty sculptural aesthetic implicit in adobe construction. One of the room's two Pueblo fireplaces is visible to the left. Outside the house still stands an adobe bake oven in perfect working order.

Above: Ceilings of split cedar saplings (*latillas*) and logs (*vigas*) are to be found in many early houses in New Mexico. The Spanish settlers were indebted to the Indians for this aesthetically pleasing and functional building technique. The ceilings in the west wing of the de Roybal House are constructed in this early manner while those of the *sala* are formed of *vigas* and pine boards, perhaps a later replacement for *latillas*.

Opposite: Approached through a handsome, spacious patio, Santa Fe's De la Peña House is inviting in every respect. The two-story porch and the balconies with carved-wood balustrades are graceful elements of the Territorial style introduced in the mid-19th century. In the interior, the massive adobe and plastered walls provide a pure sculptured backdrop for colorful art of any period; the deep window recesses channel the brilliant southwestern sunlight in dramatic shafts of unusual intensity. Abstract paintings of the modern period little resemble the traditional Indian wall hangings found in many New Mexican houses, but in this *sala* they seem as fitting and proper as the monochromatic furniture. Artificial lighting tucked into the rectangular and corbeled beams further dramatizes the display of abstract painting.

A stone sawmill dating from 1847 stands at the center of a group of buildings associated with the life and work of a 20th-century artist, Randall Davey. The setting, in the outer reaches of Santa Fe, is attractively composed. The same strong feeling of pastoral comfort is to be experienced in the old mill and its adobe additions. Except for the addition of Territorial-style embellishments, and the removal of the mill works, the center building remains virtually unchanged. Each of the two floors is given over to a large reception or living room. Stone pavers form the floor in the ground-level room shown on the opposite page; the second level floor consists of a highly-polished cement, as seen above. Ceilings in both large rooms are composed of the original wood beams and pine boards. The furnishings are dignified and appropriate for the salon of a socially-prominent painter. The ornate pier mirror and full-length tie-back draperies apply a special touch of elegance to the upper sitting room.

The full strength and appeal of the adobe method of building is realized in this Santa Fe house built during a revival of period colonial architecture in the 1920s. The term "hand-made space," applied to other buildings in northern New Mexico, might well apply to this picturesque structure. The vast *sala*, with ceilings much higher than those to be found in earlier buildings, makes use of such traditional furnishings and fittings as colorful textiles, punched-tin light fixtures, and what is known as a "shepherd's bed" above the fireplace. Although the floor plan and proportions of the building differ greatly from a colonial-period model, the revival house can be an equally satisfying and successful architectural statement. Modern construction techniques allow for a flow of inner space difficult to achieve at an earlier time.

Romantic revival styles in architecture moved during the 19th century from the East Coast to the West, from the city to the country, and slowly replaced in popularity the traditional colonial-style building. The Italianate was one popular mode which gained ascendancy in the 1840s and '50s. This front parlor from an Evanston, Illinois, home probably dates from the mid-century. It is one of several rooms of the original house which was moved in 1872 from the downtown of this early Chicago suburb to a new residential neighborhood nearby. Both the gently-curved mantel and the hearth are of marble; the firebox is of cast iron. The chandelier is set within a plaster medallion of the period. The original gas fixture was probably a great deal less ornate, but as the house grew from several to many rooms, so, too, were the lighting devices upgraded.

San Francisco is best known for its Queen Anne style homes, but nestled among them are earlier buildings which also survived the 1906 earthquake, including this residence in the Alamo Square area. Italianate in style, the home's interior was carefully restored in the 1970s to reflect its origins in the late 1860s. Woodwork is relatively simple as compared with that found in later Victorian houses; the French marble mantel, chosen for the room to replace a later model, follows the gently arched lines preferred at the time. (The original fireplace had been destroyed in the quake and replaced with a poorly-built brick monster.) As was common in the 1860s, a curved bay window projects from one side of the room, this being set off with plaster brackets at the corners. The present owners prefer contemporary furnishings and have chosen pieces with a scale and line compatible with the graceful formality of the Italianate period.

With their high towers and projecting eaves, great houses in the Italian Villa style, have suffered greatly in the 20th century. Built for wealthy patrons, they are difficult to maintain and, until recently, have suffered the opprobrium directed toward anything Victorian. Memphis, Tennessee, contains at least one fine example of such a mansion, and the rear parlor which serves as a music room is sufficient testimony to the glories of the period. The home itself dates from the 1850s, but the furnishings reflect the taste of the one family that has owned the residence since after the Civil War. With minor exceptions, the furniture, including the great breakfront cabinet, has remained unchanged since the late 19th century. Much of it was undoubtedly custom-designed for this interior.

The spacious and handsomely furnished front parlor of the Memphis house makes a splendid argument for historic preservation. The paneled ceiling was last painted many years ago and has acquired a soft patina that would be extremely difficult to reproduce. The marble mantel with pier mirror and the softly-lit bay window recess are proper period elements which also provide in this dark-paneled room a welcome brightness. The full proportions of this true villa can be seen in the exterior photograph. Visible are such typical architectural features as the arcaded loggia to the right, the great tower, the balconies, and bracketed eaves.

Above: Seen from another perspective the front parlor forms a natural part of a Victorian suite of rooms. Sliding doors with glass panels were surely kept open when entertaining visitors. Unlike modern homes with free-flowing interior spaces, those of the mid-19th century could be closed off to save heat or for privacy. Visible to the left is the entrance to an enclosed sun porch called the "Palm Room" and added around 1905.

Opposite: A small front parlor or library across the entrance hall from the room illustrated above is filled with family memorabilia. Colonel Robert Bogardus Snowden of the Confederacy dominates the room with his painted presence. The heavy brocade draperies and valences have decorated the room since at least the turn of the century. What at first appears to be a window at the left is actually an entrance leading to a side porch and porte cochere. Family members could enter this intimate room directly from the outside and, in fact, did so at least when it was the setting for funerals or other special familial events.

Little Rock's Hanger House, remodeled and doubled in size in 1889, is a full-fledged Queen Anne style residence. The "moongate arch" entryway and wrap-around porch embellish the front; a towered stair hall is seen at the right rear. The downstairs floor is remarkable for its openness and was so described by a precocious young resident in *A Visiting Girl, A Story of Little Rock Society,* at Christmas time in 1890:

> Their house was so arranged that the entire lower floor could be thrown into one room. Portiere curtains of plush usually hung between white and gold pillars, forming three large rooms, but on this occasion they were drawn aside, displaying the entire suite of rooms so admirably adapted for entertaining. Folding doors at the back of the parlors led into the saloon dining room. . . .

All the original cypress woodwork has been restored to the fresh white and gold so admired in the 1890s. This includes the fireplace which is situated to the left of the sofa. Gas has been reintroduced into the house, and the chandeliers provide a warm and fitting glow during evening hours.

Stained-glass windows filtered outside light in a practical and attractive manner in those areas of the late Victorian house which were not meant to be viewed from the outside—entrance halls, stairways, bathrooms. Most of the panels were commercially manufactured, as was this example from the Hanger House, and were widely available for use in even a modest cottage. A fine lace curtain was an extra fillip in a formal area.

Adjoining parlors—front and back—with sliding pocket doors between them are found in many homes original to the second half of the 19th century. The correspondence between the two spaces has been emphasized in this San Francisco restoration by the use of the same paper and lighting fixtures. Identical mantel and overmantel units appear in each room. The building in its present form dates from 1895, and the woodwork, all of redwood, carries the stamp of San Francisco's Eastlake period. To find it painted is by no means unusual; redwood was then a very inexpensive, common material, and was so treated. The back parlor is now serving as a dining area until restoration of an older rear portion of the house is completed.

Above: The lingering belief that Victorian interiors are gloomy and forbidding is quickly dispelled by this view of the front parlor of the San Francisco home introduced on the preceding page. Light streams through the bay window, bringing out the natural glow of the redwood and mahogany appointments. Accents of red plush upholstery and a rich oriental carpet add further highlights to the interior. The greenery of trailing plants appropriately perched on high stands is repeated in the glazed tiles of the fireplace surround.

Opposite: The library is one of two front rooms in Little Rock's Reichardt House, virtually unchanged in decoration and furnishings since 1895. Part of a residence which grew and grew in size from 1870 to 1890, these rooms were renovated throughout for a coming-out party a few years before the turn of the century. Sliding doors opening up into a central hallway allow for communication between the two rooms, each of which could serve as a parlor for entertainment. Ceiling paper, cornice decoration, and the stenciled drop have required either careful reproduction or replacement, but the essential ornamental composition and color scheme have been preserved.

The parlor stove is gone, replaced by a modern gas heater, but little else has been changed in this corner of the Reichardt House library. The fireplace is closed in with a decorative cast-iron plate; less substantial homes might have had only a painted fire board. Through the portiere to the left, one enters a back parlor now used as a dining room. The overmantel is smaller in size than one would expect in a room of such height, but it is in keeping with the natural wood tone of the moldings, doors, and furnishings. Pictures, of course, are still suspended from picture moldings.

The house began as a one-story cottage in the 1870s. The two front rooms and center hall were added eight years later, and in 1880 a kitchen and dining room wing was constructed to the right. Finally, in 1890, the house assumed its final form with the addition of a second story. The overhanging eaves, projecting center pavilion, and overall symmetrical design suggest that the owner was much more impressed with simpler styles from the past than with the still-fashionable Queen Anne.

Above: Except for a modern coffee table, a convenience for today's guests, the principal room for entertaining in the Reichardt House has been unchanged since the 1890s. The valences of wool and satin-covered balls have not been disturbed, nor have the fine lace curtains. The horsehair-covered sofa has held up over time as have other richly upholstered pieces. Four different papers are used on the walls and ceilings. The room is opened now for only special occasions as the materials used within have attained museum status and are so treasured.

Opposite: The special architectural attraction of San Francisco is its "painted ladies," Queen Anne style single-family dwellings of various sizes. The house to the right was built in the late 1890s in the Noe Valley area of the city and was a workingman's pride and joy. A front and back parlor, separated by sliding doors, provided space in which the family and guests could relax. Redwood was typically used throughout, and the fireplace surround and hearth were tiled. The restorers were fortunate to find so much of the original architectural decoration in place, including ceiling medallions and hardware.

By the early 1900s, the exuberant passions for building in the Queen Anne style had cooled considerably in San Francisco. John Anderson, a Swedish builder, constructed nearly seventy homes in the city, seven or eight of which are nearly identical to this model. While elements of the high Victorian came into play on façades, interior work reflected elements of the Colonial Revival style. The parlor shows most clearly the restrained, neoclassical spirit which prevailed within. Crown moldings appear over the door and windows, the latter being simple double-sash affairs. Partially visible is a plaster decorative design which delicately embellishes the cove ceiling. Shutters have been used to filter the strong western light.

The Colonial Revival style reached Little Rock in the 1890s and persisted in popularity across North America well through the first several decades of the 20th century. The front parlor in this home is a cool, elegant space enlivened only by the oak mantel and colorful textiles. Crown moldings set off the entryway and door to the back parlor. Applied art-nouveau decoration appears on the mantel, and above it is a graceful elliptical beveled-glass mirror. The light fixtures found on the first floor are designed to be illuminated by either electricity or by gas.

The present owners of the house have had to restore large areas, including the exterior. The second-story Palladian window is now back in place and a dormer repeating this Georgian Colonial design will soon be reinstalled. Shutters will also be hung.

The E. Arthur Davenport House (1901) in River Forest, Illinois, is one of Frank Lloyd Wright's most interesting. The master of the Prairie School style was presented with a special design problem: how to accommodate the sweeping lines, the strong horizontality of his style, on what constitutes only a 75-foot wide lot, one-half the width of the usual River Forest property. Wright's typical cruciform plan was employed, but in this case he solved his problem by merely rotating the design 90 degrees. Horizontal board-and-batten sheathing ties the center portion to the two wings. A porch that originally wrapped around the front to further emphasize the long, low profile had rotted away by 1911.

The living room is positioned in this central front portion of the house in an east-west position. It is rich with the structural detailing that characterizes Wright's work — dark stained beams and bands of woodwork which wrap around the walls and provide a visual line of communication with adjoining rooms. Built-in furniture and the bold brick fireplace compose an inviting inglenook. The present owners have let the structure speak for itself and have devoted themselves to maintaining its purity of expression.

4.
The Architectural Furnishings: Millwork, Plasterwork, and Hardware

Architectural ornamentation may set off one house in the same style from another. Although wood moldings, applied plaster decoration, and even ornamental iron have been commercially produced in an assembly-line fashion since at least the mid-19th century, the variety of forms is almost without count. And the ways in which these elements were used are even greater. This was especially true in the interior of a house where the display of personal taste was given a freer hand than on the street-side façade. While the parlor or living room has always served as a reception room for the outside world, there has rarely been restraint in its decoration. It was the parlor that was supposed to shine.

The extent of architectural elaboration reached its height in America during the second half of the 19th century. Wainscoting was usually reserved for such interiors as the main hall, kitchen, and dining room. The parlor was the place to employ ornaments from floor to ceiling, including an inventive combination of plaster or wooden moldings—a shoe molding, baseboard, chair rail, perhaps a plate rail, picture rail, and crown molding or cornice. And this was but a beginning.

Doors and windows in high Victorian interiors were defned by casings ranging from relatively flat profiles to those of great complexity. These were finished off with

"French Room"/drawing room, James A. Allison Mansion, Indianapolis, Indiana, 1911-14. The ornate plasterwork and wood moldings reflect the degree to which the homes of the very wealthy of the time were decorated in imitation of the Renaissance palaces of the Old World.

corner blocks or headblocks. Wood brackets were often tucked into the corners of doorways, and spandrels sometime linked the opening formed between sliding doors leading from one room to another. Decoration in plaster was sometimes used as well or in place of wood. Ceiling rosettes or centerpieces were standard elements from which to suspend kerosene or gas lighting fixtures; brackets at the corners of a bay-window recess were often formed of plaster; fanciful ceiling designs were worked into corners and beyond in particularly ambitious homes. Wood and plasterwork of this sort was by no means universally found; most late Victorians probably lived in relatively sober surroundings, but even these were highly ornamental in comparison with those known earlier.

The period beyond the Victorian was one of slow retreat away from such elaboration. It was also a time when classical tradition again reigned in the parlor, as it did in the Colonial and Federal periods. Some tasteful homes in the Tudor Revival style, nicknamed "stockbroker Tudor," boasted coffered plaster ceilings, fanciful ornamental wrought ironwork around windows and doorways, perhaps even boiserie or enriched wood paneling, but the general trend was back to a simplicity not known since the early 19th century.

The fine architectural detailing found in aristocratic European interiors was out of reach for most Americans in 1800-50 and earlier. Indeed, there was a strong democratic prejudice against it. Upper-class Americans did admire the Empire fashions of France, the Adamsesque neoclassicism of patrician London, and the romantic pointed "Gothick" style of early Victorian England, but execution of such foreign modes was limited in domestic building. Even Asher Benjamin, when writing of stucco designs in *The American Builder's Companion* (1806), advised that "An Ornament, however well executed, is not fit to be put in every room." The drawing room was almost alone in those interiors suggested for such treatment. A. J. Downing was even more explicit when he recommended for Americans "a tasteful simplicity of decoration, to harmonize with the character of the dwelling and its occupants."

Moldings used for windows and door-

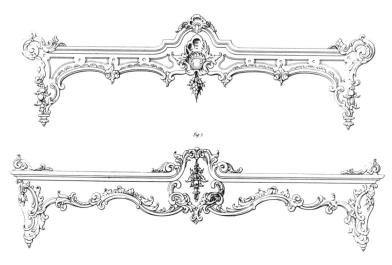

Window cornice designs from Blackie & Son, *The Cabinet Maker's Assistant, Original Designs for Furniture* (1853). Cornices of this sort were used originally only for beds and gradually moved to the window where they served a decorative purpose and a practical one of hiding the apparatus for hanging both curtains and stationary draperies.

ways were considerably flatter than the somewhat rounded profiles of the Georgian period. Wallpapers often provided the ornamental relief previously supplied by paneling and a series of different moldings. Borders and friezes could be created much more easily from a paper than from plaster or painted designs. What ornamental relief work was to be found in the early 19th-century home was probably applied only to a parlor fireplace mantel. During the Federal period it was lavished in naturalistic designs—wreaths, festoons, the acanthus; later, during the Greek Revival years of 1820 to 1840, less frivolous Greek anthemion and fret and key motives were used.

Architectural ornamentation during the previous two centuries of Colonial building followed well-articulated English designs, but of a simplified sort. Few 17th-century settlers could afford to emulate the English squirearchy and settled instead for what was considered at the time to be primitive alternatives. Horizontal wainscoting may have covered the lower section of clay-filled walls without a plaster finish. Fireplaces were often wide openings in the chimney wall without mantel or shelf. Beams were usually exposed, and corner posts, weather braces, and even timbers serving as wall studs were left naked to the eye. Although the appearance may seem charming today, it was makeshift then.

When time and money allowed, some semblance of decent decoration was applied to the basic structural elements by more sophisticated settlers. Wood was the cheapest material to use—even less expensive than paint or paper. By the early 18th century, paneled chimney breasts replaced whitewash or planking halved together. Cornices, chair rails, and bases brought the walls up to a simple Georgian Colonial

Interior window shutters, Alabama, mid-19th century. Curtains were not used in many homes until well into the 19th century, although windows were sometimes draped. For long windows reaching practically from cornice to floor, wooden louvered or paneled shutters were standard architectural furnishings.

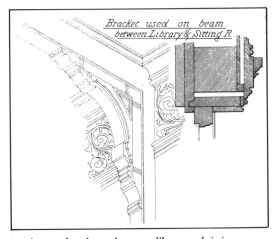

Bracket used on beam between library and sitting room, from *Modern Architectural Designs and Details* (1881) by William T. Comstock. No beam exposed in a Victorian-period house could be without some decorative appendage. The bracket served this function in the Queen Anne residence.

68

standard. Built-in cupboards provided handsome storage space. Brass appointments were rare, but earlier wooden locks and latches were being replaced with those of iron. Houses were growing in size, and the use of more sophisticated materials—brass, stucco or plaster, glass, and ceramics—was also on the increase. To decorate the parlor, however, most Americans turned in the 19th century to less expensive substitutes such as papers, paints, and textiles.

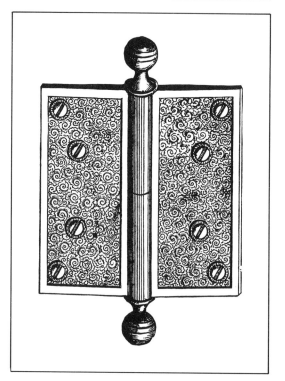

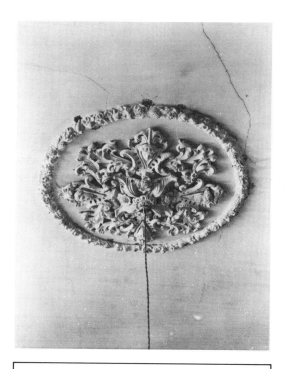

GENEVA BRONZED.
41540 Geneva Bronzed Sliding Door Latch, flat fronts; for double doors; size, 3¼x3¼ inches. Geneva bronze front and strike, bronze bolt, complete with 4 elongated flush Geneva bronzed escutcheons, one set in a box; weight, 4½ pounds.
Per set.........$0.80

Opposite page. Left (top): Plaster ceiling medallion, Alabama, 19th century. Centerpieces became standard in the well-appointed parlor early in the 1800s. The designs were numerous throughout the country. *Left (bottom):* Sliding-door latch, from Montgomery Ward & Co. catalogue, 1895. Victorian double parlor doors required special hardware that allowed for easy movement—tracks and latches equipped will pulls. *Right (top):* Butt hinge, from advertisement for Russell & Erwin Manufacturing Co., New Britain, Connecticut, 1881. Even such a device featured stamped decoration of a fanciful sort in the late 19th century. *Right (bottom):* Electric light and combination gas fixture, advertisement for the Edison General Electric Co., 1891. The model shown is a bracket type; similar devices were available at the time for use as center hanging fixtures.

This page. Top: Floor register plate, Villard House, New York City, McKim, Meade and White, architects, 1882-86. Movement of hot air from one room to another required the use of floor register plates. Such registers, often with highly ornamental designs, were first used with simple heating systems tied in with the parlor stove, as illustrated on page 18. *Center:* Designs for ceiling ornaments, from Asher Benjamin, *The American Builder's Companion* (1806 and following editions). The stucco designs for centerpieces partake of the delicate neoclassical spirit popular at the time. *Bottom:* Plaster cornice designs, from A. J. Downing, *The Architecture of Country Houses* (1850). That at left was recommended for "cottages in any modified Grecian or Italian forms"; at right, for "cottages in the Gothic style."

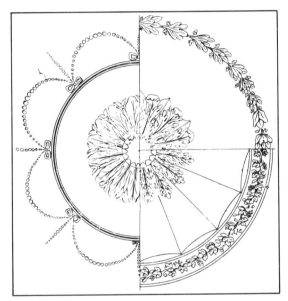

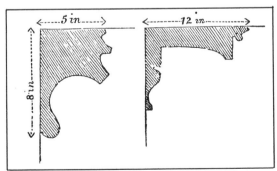

Parlor, Joseph Collins House, near West Chester, Pennsylvania, 1727. The original part of a one-room-deep dwelling was remodeled in 1758-60 to include a small "parlor" fireplace rather than a large cooking space. The placement of a drawer in the window reveal is found in other southeastern Pennsylvania houses of the period.

Southeast drawing-room wall, "Westover," near Charles City, Virginia, 1730-34. Built for William Byrd II, "Westover" was designed as a Georgian Colonial house following details provided by English architectural books. The monumental marble mantel is worthy of the best Georgian country houses in England. The classical detailing of the walls and windows is similarly accomplished.

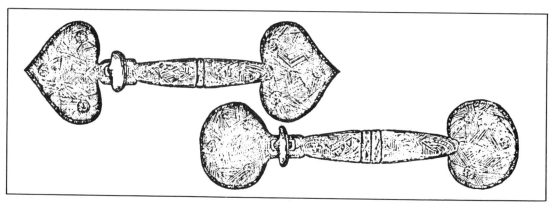

Interior door latches, The Hampton Hospital House, Camden County, New Jersey, 18th century. Handmade thumb latches of wrought iron are typical in design of those used well into the early 1800s, when they were gradually replaced by cast-iron machine-made products.

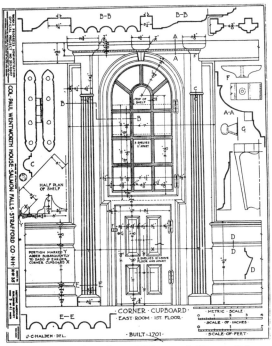

Corner cupboard, Col. Paul Wentworth House, Salmon Falls, New Hampshire, 1701. A measured drawing from the Historic American Buildings Survey archives gives the precise dimensions and profiles of one of the Colonial period's most popular and copied architectural furnishings.

Parlor, "Oaklands," Gardiner, Maine, 1835-37, designed by Richard Upjohn. The mantel with a gentle Tudor arch, and the window composed of one fixed sash above and a casement below, are typical of the architectural furnishings of this superb Gothic Revival house. The painted scenic paper is unusual for this or any other country home of the period.

Parlor, John Parke House, Parkesburg, Pennsylvania, c. 1846. Most residents of rural 19th-century America could not afford fancy woodwork or plasterwork and left their walls bare except for a finish of whitewash, kalsomine, or a cheap wallpaper. Itinerant painters, who could simulate the effect of more expensive ornamentation, however, were available in many areas. Louis Mader, one such itinerant, painted murals and trompe l'oeil woodwork and trim in this and in a second room. Such a painter was also able to simulate a marble dado.

5.
Paints, Papers, and Fabrics

Aparlor or living room in any period has been the place where family, friends, and neighbors have been entertained. Architects and builders realized how important the parlor was to the owners of a home and specified the finest appointments affordable. The principal room, A. J. Downing wrote, "should always exhibit more beauty and elegance than any apartment in the house." During the 1800s the finest papers were to be used here; oil paint was recommended over whitewash or a kalsomine treatment; oak, ash, cherry, maple, and mahogany might be used for woodwork rather than pine; carpeting and large-size rugs were preferred to a few scattered homemade floor coverings or painted wood floors.

"Curtains in the style mores of our time," William Seale has commented in *Recreating the Historic House Interior,* "compensate for the lack of interior architectural detailing." An expert on historic interiors, he is, of course, right about the tendency today to substitute mere makeup for substance. But somewhat the same situation has prevailed throughout much of American history. During the post-Civil War period, for instance, the draping of windows, doors, and furniture reached extravagant heights, suggesting perhaps that the housewife wished to hide undistin-

guished mass-produced woodwork and machine-turned furniture from the view of her guests. Similarly, as Clarence Cook complained in *The House Beautiful* (1881), the use of wall-to-wall carpeting was necessary because "Even in our best New-York houses the floors are meanly laid. . . ." Papers were recommended in earlier years of the century because they conveniently covered up mortared walls which had not been provided with a hard finish of plaster of Paris. Horizontal paper borders were used to hide the tag ends of larger vertical panel papers. All of this may not have been true of the very best of American homes, buildings designed by persons of wealth, but the general lack of architectural finishing of a fine sort is well documented by contemporary American critics as well as by European visitors.

In the 17th and 18th centuries there was less time to devote to surface decoration, and both paint and paper—the handiest tools of the interior decorator, lay or professional—were beyond the means of most families. The architectural styles of these centuries, however, emphasized architectural elements and not surface finishes. The general level of workmanship, still maintained by craftsmen and not salaried factory workers, was of a higher sort than it was to be in later years. Tongue-

Top: There is hardly a single element without applied decoration in this Victorian parlor of the late 1800s. Virtually nothing is left uncovered with fabric, paper, wood, or knickknacks. *Above:* The fashionable early-Victorian parlor was a model of restrained elegance in comparison with the late-Victorian. One wallpaper allowed the home owner to simulate a cornice and wall panels.

and-groove paneling, for instance, was cheaper to install than an imported scenic paper from France. The handiwork of the inventive Colonial artisan, forced by economic necessity to be imaginative and enterprising, is rightly admired today as it has been since the Colonial Revival of the 1890s and early 1900s. The honesty of materials and their skillful, straight-forward use appeal to us today when merchandise is recalled almost as soon as it is produced.

Judgments on the past, however, are only useful if they are based on an understanding of the taste of a period, the kinds of values and standards which guided the home decorator and builder, and the economic conditions of the time. No one is about to faithfully restore an interior considered truly horrendous in color, pattern, and proportion. On the other hand, in order to interpret successfully any particular style, one must study the mediocre as well as the splendid, the well-planned and the accidental. Every period has its tasteful interludes, and although we may prefer one to another, each has something to recommend it. This is as true of what we now consider the overstuffed parlor of the "brown decades" of 1865-95, as it is of the comfortable drawing room of a Georgian Colonial home of the 1750s.

A. J. Downing, reacting to the severe aesthetics of neoclassical decorative schemes, recommended that the drawing room be painted or papered in a color "lighter, more cheerful and gay, than any other room. The furniture should be richer and more delicate in design, and the colors of the walls decidedly light, so that brilliancy of effect is not lost in the evening." He was also aware of differences in style between a country and a city home. "In town houses, white, relieved by gold, is preferred; but in country houses, gilding should be very sparingly used—and very delicate tints, such as ashes of rose, pearl-gray, pale apple-green, etc., have a more chaste and satisfactory effect for the side walls—relieved by darker shades for the contrast." In his appeals Downing was hardly more successful than those architectural critics of the time who begged farmers to give their homes something other than a white coat of paint, but some people obviously did hear his message. These were the fashion leaders and those who have left behind for us the best examples of mid-Victorian interior design.

Downing and all other writers on home building and decoration of his time recommended the use of papers, then being mass produced for the first time. He was aware of the lack of architectural distinction in most American homes and felt that it could be corrected through the sub-

stitution of an appropriate paper. "A cornice adds very considerably to the architectural character of any room, though it is seldom or never introduced in cheap cottages, except, perhaps, in a parlor or best room. When the walls are papered, its place is in a good degree supplied by the border, representing a cornice on the paper itself." The fashion for French paneled papers in the 1860s and '70s was based on a similar longing for a handsome effect, in this case one that would have been created by molded and gilded woodwork of the European salon of Louis XV. Special ceiling papers which simulated plaster ornamentation and a centerpiece were also available. In the same vein, the flocked handmade papers used in fine Georgian Colonial homes of one-hundred years earlier imitated the use of rich fabrics as wall coverings.

Wallpaper became such a common

Left: Parlor, Ruggles House, Columbia Falls, Maine, 1818, designed by Aaron Simmons Sherman. The elaborate woodwork with mahogany inlays displayed in this Federal-style room requires little in the way of further embellishment. Not visible in this photograph is an elaborate cornice molding. Both the use of paper and fabric is very restrained. The woodwork is painted an off-white. *Right:* Drawing room cornice, Devereaux House (Staines-Jennings Mansion), Salt Lake City, Utah, 1857, enlarged 1867, William Paul, architect. Just how elaborate a wall treatment could become in the last half of the 19th century is only suggested here.

commodity in 19th-century America that it was used in the parlor to simulate cornices, friezes, and panels, and it was used in the form of such late 19th-century heavy textured pattern papers as Lincrusta-Walton and leather papers, to imitate wainscoting or a stuccoed dado. Home restorers today should not be surprised to find remnants of old patterns on closet walls; paper became so inexpensive that it could be used even in hidden spaces. Anyone seeking evidence of what was used in years past is well advised to search out such out of the way places in the house.

Until the 1870s French patterns in papers were the most popular. The use of such materials had been limited during the Colonial period by their expense, and, with the perfection of steam-powered presses in the 1830s, the whole world seemed to blossom out in color. There were, of course, the so-called plain papers available for subdued neoclassical parlors, but printing could create much more exciting effects in the 1850s and '60s in keeping with the taste for Rococo Revival and Renaissance Revival furnishings in rich walnut and other fine-grained hardwoods. The papers were of two sorts: strongly contrasting color combinations in stripes and large realistic floral designs, and more muted papers with small patterns in imitation of damasks and silks. The abstract floral patterns so often identified today with the Victorian period, the designs of William Morris and his studio, only came into public favor in the late 1870s.

Use of fabrics followed a similar course of development, improvements in their printing and weaving making them more and more affordable beginning in the late 18th century. Earlier than this, most tex-

Back parlor, "Roseland," Woodstock, Connecticut, mid-19th century. The heavily-embossed paper used below the border was imported from England in the 1860s and is dark green on a cream-color ground. A novelty at the time in America, this material was known as Lincrusta Walton and was manufactured later in the United States as well.

tiles were woven and handmade and of a very simple sort. Windows were often not covered in any way, and parlor floors were usually left bare or sparsely furnished with a few scatter rugs made from rags and remnants. Bed hangings were likely to be the most lavish of the textiles to appear in a home, and if the grownups' bedstead was still to be found in the parlor—as it might have been at the time—rather than in a special bed chamber, the room presented a display of color and texture that not even window curtains or draperies could begin to match. Furniture was rarely upholstered.

The Colonial style so admired today is that form known as Georgian. In America it was indulged during the 18th century by any family that could afford such a fashionable step forward. Tab curtains of linen, linsey-woolsey, or cotton were hung at windows, or, in more ambitious homes, larger-sized windows were draped with brilliantly-colored calicoes and chintzes or even silks. Cotton muslin was sometimes used as a lining. Cushions were introduced for seating furniture, and the upholstered wing chair with its inviting and protective high back and sides was brought down from the bedroom to the parlor. It is difficult to believe today that such a form as the wing chair originally would have been considered informal, but ease was introduced to the "best" room slowly.

Window treatments became more and more elaborate during the 19th century, beginning with festoons which hung down in somewhat the manner of Austrian shades but with much less regularity and without scallops. Curtains which could be rolled down over the window or divided down the middle were basically an 18th-century development, an accommodation to the use of sash windows rather than casements. It became de rigueur to tie these

Opposite page. Top: A mid-19th-century paper in an early-1800s Florence, Alabama, home redecorated in the Renaissance Revival style. *Bottom:* Southwest parlor, Governor Henry Lippitt House, Providence, Rhode Island, 1862-65, Henry Childs, architect. The walls were covered with a light-colored geometric-patterned paper now almost completely faded from view. A much more elaborate wall covering was used in the adjoining library, visible at left.

This page. Top: A wallpaper designed and recommended by Charles L. Eastlake in his *Hints on Household Taste in Furniture, Upholstery and Other Details* (1878) and manufactured by Jeffrey & Co. Eastlake was instrumental in popularizing the designs of William Morris and his studio. *Bottom:* A late-19th-century paper and frieze based on "Peony," a semi-naturalistic design attributed to the Morris studio.

back in some fashion, and eventually the pole from which they hung was hidden by a valance and a lambrequin. Gimp, fringe, and tassels were added to draperies which, as William Seale reminds us, were considered "valances or any feature of a window hanging sewn to hang in a stationary configuration of folds." Draperies hung over curtains, which may or may not have hung in turn over shades or roller blinds.

The materials most often identified with the Victorian parlor are velvet plush and lace. Both, however, were later 19th-century replacements for such fabrics as horsehair and woolen stuffs. "Lace," Seale has found, "was as indispensable to the elegant drawing room of the 1870s as it was in the 1880s to the pretty parlor of a modest row house. In the first it was probably used with heavy side curtains, which were tied back, leaving the field of lace to pattern the light from the windows." In more modest dwellings, he adds, "the lace might hang by itself, either run on a rod through a casing or rings, or banded at the top by a cornice."

English designer and architect Charles Eastlake, who has been blamed wrongly for many of the excesses of Victorian home decorators, found the whole practice of hiding the tops of draperies or curtains behind cornices and/or lambrequins quite ridiculous. He also decried the heavy use of fringe, reminding the readers of *Hints on Household Taste* that "Fringe, as Pugin justly pointed out, was originally nothing more than the threads of silk or woollen stuff knotted together at a ragged edge, to prevent it from unravelling further. By degrees they came to be knotted at regular intervals, so that at length this contrivance grew into a system of ornament which survived the necessity of its original adoption."

Eastlake was one of many critics who

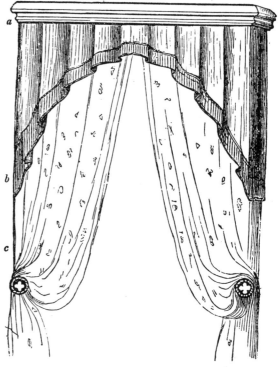

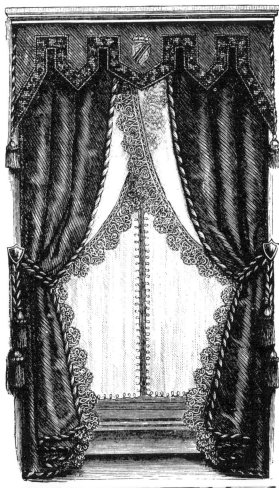

Opposite page. Top: Drapery with blind, parlor, General R. E. Jones House, Alabama, mid-19th century, photograph dates from the 1930s. Extended windows were sometimes fitted with a base below which could be opened or closed, depending on the weather. The drapery was to remain stationary and was not intended to be looped over the ladder-back chair. *Bottom:* A. J. Downing's suggested window treatment in *The Architecture of Country Houses* (1850) with (a) cornice, (b) drapery, and (c) curtains.

This page. Top: Four layers of material and a cornice from which to hang it were recommended by Henry T. Williams and Mrs. C. S. Jones in *Beautiful Homes or Hints in House Furnishing* (1878). *Bottom:* Painted blind, Captain John Hart-Milton House, Eufala, Alabama, mid-19th century. "Nothing can be more vulgar and tawdry," Downing wrote in 1850, "than most of the transparencies and painted curtains. . . . ." Obviously, many Victorians disagreed.

influenced the public away from what was considered over-decoration in the last quarter of the 19th century. The movement toward simplicity was to culminate in the revivals of English and Spanish Colonial styles. Although windows were by this time much larger than most found in many pre-19th-century homes and were quickly being converted in many homes from small-paned affairs to large plates of glass, less covering of them was considered more healthful and attractive. Curtains or draperies, all the critics said, could be hung from turned rods by means of brass rings. Similarly, they urged the removal of fringe from upholstered furniture where, in Eastlake's words, "no one but a modern upholsterer would ever think of putting it."

The history of the use of floor coverings follows a course much like that of window hangings and papers. Wall-to-wall carpeting had become an American indulgence early in the 1800s. With the advent of new facilities of mass production, carpeting of this sort was as affordable for the average household as wallpaper produced in continuous rolls. Wiltons, Brussels, and ingrain carpets were manufactured in a multitude of patterns and color combinations, the darkest of which were usually recommended for reasons of wear and because the deep color—in combination with light walls and woodwork—added visual size to a room. Not until after the Civil War was the practice of using wall-to-wall covering attacked as being wasteful, unhealthy, and unattractive. With the introduction of better hardwood flooring in the 1870s, it became unseemly to hide the floor completely. High-quality oriental rugs soon captured the market for expensive floor coverings, and these and cheaper domestic imi-

Left: A Gothic archway which set off a bay window alcove presented a special problem for the housewife who wished to drape architectural features. In the William M. Spencer House (c. 1850), Galiopolis, Alabama, a carved wooden cornice covered with fabric was tortuously fitted into place.

Opposite page (left): Clarence Cook's suggestion for hanging a curtain or portiere in *The House Beautiful* (1881) was to place it "in line with the spring of the arch itself, leaving the whole arch open for light and air."

tations continued in popularity well into the 20th century. There was also a parallel revival of interest in Colonial-period hooked and braided rag rugs, the use of which had survived in rural areas.

The use of paint in the parlor was limited at first to small decorative touches such as woodwork and spattered or stenciled walls and floors. Whitewash was most likely the closest many early settlers came to a decorative finish. Oil paints did not adhere well to the roughly-finished walls of many homes, and what paint was available was saved for woodwork. Contrary to the belief born of the Colonial Revival, woodwork was not painted white but could be decorated in a fairly wide range of colors produced from natural dyes and pigments. These colors are well known today because of the research done at such historic villages as Colonial Williamsburg, Sturbridge, and

their counterparts across the country.

Beginning in the mid-18th century and lasting well into the next in popularity was the practice of stenciling designs on walls and floors. In the early 1800s these were often applied around windows and doors and as a border or a frieze beneath a real or fake cornice. As long as papers could not be purchased economically, the art of stenciling flourished, particularly in rural areas. In the cities, wall decorations were often the work of more talented painters who applied whole scenes to well plastered and perhaps canvassed surfaces.

Paint colors employed during the first half of the 19th century began in various light, airy, almost pastel shades of blue, green, and red which blended well with the delicate, formal appointments of the Federal or Empire parlor; white was preferred for woodwork. Gradually the wall colors

"Curtains for an Every-day Window" were recommended by Cook to be hung on plain brass rings and rod.

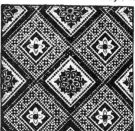

For illustration showing the exact colorings see page 894. At 23 cents per yard for one-yard width to 46 cents per yard for two-yard width we offer this rich, handsome pattern of heavy weight, extra strong floor oilcloth. This is one of the greatest values ever shown. It is very low in price but the quality will prove to be extraordinary. It is one the greatest values ever shown by any house. This oilcloth is made for us under contract by one of the best makers in this country. The color effects, pattern and material that are used in its construction are closely inspected by our buyer for this department. We have reduced the price to the actual cost of the labor and material and to this we add but our one small percentage of profit. If it is not entirely satisfactory, a greater value than you could get elsewhere for double the money, you have the privilege of returning it and your money will be refunded. Width, yards....... 1 1½ 2

No. 37R1941 Price, per yard.......23c 35c 46c

Floor oilcloth offered by Sears, Roebuck and Co., in 1902. Such material could have been used as a protective covering over a rug or carpet in the area of the hearth or on a center table.

View from sitting room to dining room, The Black House, Ellsworth, Maine, 1824-27. Wall-to-wall carpeting is overlaid with area rugs. The carpeting is obviously not of the early 19th century, but such an elegant home would have included such overall floor covering in the principal first-floor rooms. The design of the house is based almost entirely on a plan first published by Asher Benjamin in *The American Builder's Companion* (1806).

darkened as did the furniture and woodwork. Paint was used more often on wall areas and not on woodwork, thus reversing the Colonial practice. While the woodwork in less important rooms might be painted white, that of the best rooms, the parlor and dining room in particular, called for the display of fine wood. French polish, a varnish, heightened natural wood effects and those which had been imitated by means of graining.

The variety of colors available to the Victorian decorator increased each year. Magenta was introduced in 1859, and deep blues and greens were popular. Finally, before a return to lighter shades in the 1890s, there was great interest in the colors used by such widely-admired English painters of the pre-Raphaelite school as Alma-Tadema, Burne-Jones, Rossetti, and Morris. As described by Clarence Cook in *The*

House Beautiful, these were "mistletoe green, the blue green, the duck's egg, the rose-amber, the pomegranate-flower." Such shades, however, required special mixing, and most Americans after 1870, when ready-mixed paints first became available, opted for convenience and low cost. This meant more neutral, sober colors. The greater ease by which paints could be bought and used, however, led to their much more frequent use. By the turn of the century, the highly-colored wallpaper patterns of the Victorians, whether naturalistic cabbage roses or the sophisticated semi-naturalistic designs of the English, were considered decidedly old-fashioned by the trend setters. From that time on, to redecorate a parlor or living room meant first of all to give it a fresh coat of paint, woodwork and all.

6.
Furnishing the Period Living Room and Parlor

As the most important room in a house, the parlor or living room has been furnished more lavishly than any other. In the words of a late Victorian enthusiast, the parlor "should be a room full of beauty and brightness, testifying at once to the large and generous hospitality, as well as to the taste and wise discrimination of the queen-mistress who reigns over the realm of which this is the state chamber." The "queen-mistress" often drove her husband to drink with all her fussing about the room, but no one could fault her for not caring enough for the comfort and social appearance of her family. The parlor has been considered the center of all that was most civilized in almost any given period of the history of the American home. Children learned, if possible, to stay away from it, but they, too, as adults, came to live in houses with such a "best" room.

In the early Colonial period, anything approximating a stylistically consistent set of furnishings was rarely encountered. Rather, a room was likely to include a collection of pieces prized more for their utility than for their decorative qualities. Consequently, it is questionable whether a "set" look is truly an authentic one for many period homes of the early years of settlement. Not until the mid-19th century did suites of furniture become at all common in the parlor. Even so, pieces of the same stylistic period are not an absolute must in an old house; modern art and furnishings can often be used effectively with the antique.

As mentioned previously, the most imposing object in the early parlor might have been a four-poster bed with hangings, the specialized bed chamber or room being a later addition in many dwellings. Found along with the bed were such useful objects as chests, stools, a trestle table, and perhaps several turned chairs. A special possession would have been a turned chair with arms, a carved "wainscot" chair with high back. The room might also have included a bench, with or without a back. Upholstered furniture was virtually unknown in the 17th century. The general appearance was one of sparseness, an effect relieved only by a possible table covering and the bedstead's curtains.

Settlers of greater wealth, especially in the southeastern tidewater regions, brought with them fancier furnishings and patronized craftsmen who could fashion new pieces. City dwellers also advanced more rapidly in the acquisition of fine furnishings than did the majority of the population who lived in the country. Until the early 1700s, however, skilled cabinetmakers and chairmakers were limited in number and skill throughout the colonies. Few fortunes were sufficient to allow for the importation of sets of matching chairs and fine tables. Oak and pine were the predominant medium for well-executed furniture in the 1700s.

The gently-curved Queen Anne style was transmitted to the colonies in the early 18th century along with plans for homes in the Georgian style. By the 1760s, Chippendale designs were being used alongside the Queen Anne in furniture. In the last quarter of the century, George Hepplewhite's and Thomas Sheraton's designs were eagerly added to the portfolio of fine furniture makers whose number had increased greatly from the mid-century. Workshops in Boston, Newport, New London, New York, Philadelphia, Annapolis, Baltimore, Williamsburg, Richmond, and Charleston could produce extraordinarily handsome high- and lowboys, chests-on-chests, sets of wing and side chairs, sofas, secretaries, tilt-top, tray-top, drop-leaf, and card tables which were handsome additions to any parlor. It should be remembered, however, that most Americans of the time lived far from the centers of fashion; the furnishings of their "best" room were far from the sophisticated sort deemed fitting in the city. The same situation prevailed throughout the 19th century.

Furniture forms in the early 1800s assumed more classical lines. The Grecian armchair with a flat broad crest rail and scrolled arms is representative of the sort of object that might have been found in a dignified Federal or Greek Revival parlor; the lyre-back side chair from the New York studio of Duncan Phyfe is yet another familiar form. Woods such as cherry, lightly-stained mahogany, maple, and fruitwood were popular, and special pieces were inlaid with veneer, gilded, or provided with

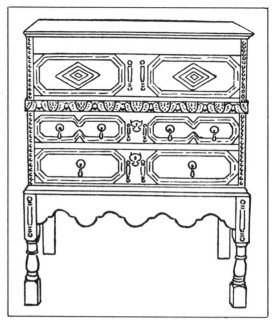

Oak chest with drawers, c. 1670. Furniture, termed "Pilgrim Century" in later years, was massive in form, often carved, and decorated with symbolic motifs.

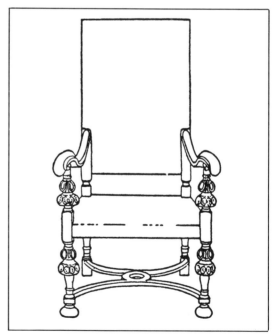

Upholstered square-back armchairs of this sort, transitional in style from the Pilgrim Century to the Queen Anne, were prized possessions in a prosperous early-18th-century household.

Windsor chairs were commonly used in American homes from the early 18th century and were made in many different forms; at far left is another furniture style — the Queen Anne — which remained popular in the Colonies far longer than it did in England, its place of origin.

A sofa with outscrolled arms and a plain crest rail was a fashionable piece for an early-19th-century parlor. Both the sofa and chairs with curved backs and scrolled arms were among those pieces of furniture termed "Grecian" in the 1800s.

Southeast parlor, The Black House, Ellsworth, Maine, 1824-27. Although the house itself is Federal in style, the interior reflects both in its appointments and furnishings a much wider range of time. The Black family lived here until 1928, and since that time the house has been furnished with a mix of Colonial and Victorian pieces, as it would have been in the mid-19th century.

Opposite page. Left (top): Parlor, "Camden Place," Port Royal vicinity, Virginia, 1856-59, N. G. Starkwether, architect. A rococo parlor set of the type illustrated here was usually made of rosewood and included a console table, as seen in the corner, and a center table. Both pieces would have been supplied with marble tops. Reflected in the ornate mirror is a matching sofa. The carpeting and draperies are also original furnishings. *Left (middle):* Front parlor, Henry Marvin Yerington House, Carson City, Nevada, c. 1870, as photographed in 1889. This Victorian parlor was relatively modest in its furnishings. The windows were not heavily draped and the furniture is free of heavy upholstery. There is, however, a great deal of what today's homemaker would term "clutter": an easel holding two pictures, one partially draped; a parlor piano, also decorated with fabric; and a generous supply of occasional tables or stands. *Left (bottom):* A "sitting-room" rocker from *Beautiful Homes Or Hints in House Furnishing* (1878) by Henry T. Williams and Mrs. C. S. Jones. There were thousands of models proposed for use in the parlor or sitting room during the 1800s, each one of which featured some extra item of comfort. *Right (top):* "Much in Little Space," from *The House Beautiful* (1881) by Clarence Cook. The use of straightforward "Eastlake" furniture, Cook believed, added to an attractive, aesthetically-pleasing look. *Right (middle):* The whatnot or *étagère,* as illustrated in A. J. Downing's *The Architecture of Country Houses* (1850), was a staple of Victorian parlor furnishings. *Right (bottom):* Parlor, Jeremiah Nunan House, Jacksonville, Oregon, 1891-92, designed by George Franklin Barber. This late-19th-century interior is decidedly eclectic in design and furnishing and, as seen today, reflects a turning away from the use of the matching set or suite, a practice popular from the 1840s through the '70s. The tiled fireplace, mantel, and overmantel with turned balusters supporting shelves and a decorative cornice are representative of the Queen Anne style popular in the 1880s and '90s. The ceiling fixture is electric and probably original to the house.

bronze mounts. The Récamier couch with one scrolled end higher than the other was added to many parlors and is a reminder of the growing influence of French furniture designs.

A center table with a pedestal base was first introduced in the parlor during these years, and there it would stay—in one form or another—until at least the end of the century. This fixture William Seale has termed the "family altar." Here the family could gather in the evening for prayers or reading as the table was always supplied with light, at least an oil lamp; often it was illuminated by a hanging lantern or chandelier. Marble tops were common at first for this type of table and for other pieces supplied by a cabinetmaker. By the mid-1800s it was thought necessary for the center table to be draped, for as Downing commented, "Both sofa and centre tables depend for their good effect mainly on the drapery or cover of handsome cloth or stuff usually spread upon their tops, and concealing all but the lower part of the legs." Downing was expressing a general distaste for the unyielding lines of Empire furnishings and a desire for the more romantic treatment then fashionable in England and on the Continent. "How often does the interior of the same house convey to us a totally different impression," he wrote,

when inhabited and furnished by different families. In the one case, all is cold, hard, and formal as solid mahogany and marble-top centre-tables, alias, bare conventionalities and frigid social feeling, can make it; in the other, all is as easy and agreeable as low couches, soft light chintzes and cushions—alias, cordiality, and genuine, frank hospitality can render it.

Downing especially favored use of the Gothic style in furniture, the black walnut or rosewood side chair with cusped-arch back being a common example. Also popular were cabinets or cupboards with such

88

Gothic motifs as quatrefoils, trefoils, rosettes, heraldic devices, crockets, and arches. By the mid-century, furniture was beginning to assume more of a rounded shape than the pointed Gothic. Upholstery was substituted for open tracery in chairs and sofas. Carved ornament in the 18th-century Louis XV style—curving lines and scrolls—topped or surrounded backs and frames. Much of this furniture came to be produced in factories, and its quality was questioned by the experts in interior design of the time. Simpler "cottage" or parlor sets of pine which could be stained and varnished were frequently recommended over the more elaborate. By the 1880s, it would not have been difficult to find many people who agreed with Clarence Cook's observation:

The tendency is to crowd our rooms beyond their capacity, by which we make ourselves very uncomfortable, and destroy the value, as decoration, of many pieces, and their real usefulness as articles of furniture. What with easels, chairs not meant for use, little teetery stands, pedestals, and the rest of the supernumerary family filling up the room left by the solid and supposed useful pieces, it is sometimes a considerable test of one's dexterity and presence of mind to make one's way from end to end of a long New York drawing-room. Mignon's egg dance was as nothing to it.

The overdecorating was partly a result of a desire to make the parlor as cozy, warm, and comfortable as possible. The rocking chair, for instance, became a standard item after it slowly made its way from the bedroom to the new informality of the parlor, and its proportions increased over the years after the introduction of platform models. The general mid- and late-Victorian approach to the decoration of the parlor was well summed up by Henry T. Williams and Mrs. C. S. Jones in their phenomenally successful *Beautiful Homes, or Hints in House Furnishings* (1878) which was

chock-full of do-it-yourself projects: "Let this room [the living room] . . . be the first to receive attention; and here bring the pretty home-made knick knacks which give such an air of cosy comfort. . . . By such little devices, men are frequently brought to take an interest in home affairs, and this is not a feeling to quickly die out, but is rather one that luxuriates and grows by feeding." The étagère or whatnot, in elaboration varying from simple spool turnings to tortured fretwork, was the kind of object useful for the display of souvenirs, photographs, family china. The mantel was also a favorite resting place for such artistic objects, as was a towering overmantel with built-in shelves for bric-a-brac.

Edith Wharton and Oliver Codman thought they understood the cause of what they termed "the general craving for knickknacks." It was "the reaction from the bare stiff rooms of the first quarter of the present [19th] century—the era of mahogany and horsehair. . . ." They were, in part, correct, but there were other reasons just as important. More money was available to spend on decorative items; the display of what in its time was considered to be *objets d'art* was thought to provide a moral, uplifting influence; and there was a decided increase in the variety of furnishings offered for sale, most of them the products of machines and not craftsmen. Despite the entreaties of Clarence Cook in 1881 and Wharton and Codman nearly twenty years later, the turning away from the overstuffed and overdecorated proceeded slowly.

The first reaction to the excess of ornamentation can be seen in the adoption of Eastlake-style furnishings in the 1880s and '90s. Although supplied with turnings and panels, these pieces—typically black walnut, oak, or pine occasional tables and armchairs with incised designs — are considerably plainer than their Rococo and Renaissance Revival predecessors. Eastlake's designs were often called "Jacobean" in style and do resemble, at least in weight, pieces from the early 17th century.

Closer to a model of simplicity acceptable to such purists as Wharton and Codman in the late 1890s are pieces based on late-17th and 18th-century English and Continental designs. These critics applauded the emergence of the Colonial Revival, although many aspects of its execution by commercial furniture makers were thoroughly deplored. So-called Queen Anne side chairs with stamped paneled backs were, indeed, a far cry from the early 18th-century carved models with hoop-shaped backs and vase-shaped splats.

Simpler forms such as the arts-and-crafts Morris chair, Mission oak tables and square boxy chairs, and Craftsman desks did prevail in many fashionable circles throughout the country by the 1920s. Also popular in the parlor were true antiques from the Colonial and Federal periods, some retrieved from country attics in what was to be a continuing 20th-century obsession — collecting. The 1920s also saw the beginning of the preservation and restoration movement in architecture, for what to do with all these old belongings? Proper settings for them had to be discovered or fabricated. Whole period rooms were acquired by the wealthy, and a number of these settings are now found in public museums or villages. The average person retrieved family possessions from the attic and, in time, sought to provide a congenial setting for their display.

OUR $17.55 GENUINE TURKISH THREE-PIECE PARLOR SUITE.

"A Genuine Turkish Three-Piece Parlor Suite" of the sort thoroughly detested by Eastlake and Cook, and widely admired by many American housewives in the late-Victorian period. From Sears, Roebuck & Co.'s 1902 catalogue.

THIS ELEGANT THREE-PIECE TURKISH PARLOR SUITE consists of one tete-a-tete, one gents' easy chair, and one parlor or reception chairs, three pieces, and all these pieces are made in extra large size, with extra high backs and large comfortable seats, and are the very latest designs. The upholstering or covering of this suite is the latest design or pattern of imported goods; each piece is covered with a different color; the suite is beautifully upholstered with tufted plush bands on upper backs, and trimmed with a heavy worsted fringe. The suite is made with the best springs and spring edges, and every piece is made with spring back. This is, without doubt, one of the best parlor suites put on the market at the price we ask, and will be an ornament to any home.
YOU WOULD GET NOTHING FINER if you were to go to the best store in the city and pay double the price.

PRICES FOR COMPLETE SUITE OF THREE PIECES, SOFA, ARM CHAIR AND RECEPTION CHAIR:

No. 1R6060	Upholstered in High Colored Velours	$17.55
No. 1R6062	Upholstered in French Gobelin Tapestry	18.60
No. 1R6064	Upholstered in Crushed Plush	19.70
No. 1R6066	Upholstered in Mercerized Tapestry	20.10
No. 1R6058	Upholstered in Silk Brocatelle	22.25
No. 1R6070	Upholstered in Silk Damask	23.65

PRICES FOR SINGLE PIECES:

	Colored Velours	French Gobe- lin Tapestry	Crushed Plush	Mercerized Tapestry	Silk Brocatelle	Silk Damask
Sofa	$8.40	$8.85	$9.25	$9.45	$10.60	$10.95
Arm Chair	5.40	5.80	6.30	6.40	7.25	7.85
Rocker	6.15	6.45	6.95	7.10	8.10	8.40
Reception Chair	3.75	3.95	4.15	4.25	4.70	4.85

The classic center table was also known as a "pillar table." Sears' 1902 model was made of oak, weighed 150 pounds, and sold, in the 8-foot-diameter size, for $8.70.

Illustration Credits

In this list of illustration credits, sources not specifically identified in the captions are given. The following abbreviations are used: a (above), b (below), m (middle), t (top), l (left), and r (right). Illustrations from the archives of the Historic American Buildings Survey (now part of the National Architectural and Engineering Record) housed at the Library of Congress are identified as LC-HABS. Those still housed at HABS are so designated. Illustrations from the Library of Congress collections are abbreviated as LC.

Cover/jacket: Eric Schweikardt (l,a); Michael Kanouff (l,b and r,a); Allison Abraham (r,b).

P. 1, HABS; p. 2, HABS, Jack E. Boucher; p. 5, LC-HABS; p. 7, HABS.

Introduction: p. 10, HABS, Richard Cheek (l), LC, Farm Security Administration, Russell Lee (r).

1. *The Living Room and Parlor: A History:* p. 11, HABS, Jack E. Boucher; p. 12, LC (l), LC-HABS (r); p. 13, LC-HABS (l and r); p. 14, HABS, Jack E. Boucher (t), LC-HABS (b); p. 15, LC-HABS (t), *Early American Rooms, 1650-1858* (1936) by Russell Hawes Kettell; p. 17, LC; p. 18, LC-HABS (t,l), *The Art Journal Illustrated Catalogue, The Industry of Nations 1851* (l); p. 20, *Period Furnishings* (1914) by C. R. Clifford; p. 21, *The Art Journal Illustrated Catalogue, The Industry of Nations 1851;* p. 22, LC-HABS, Jack E. Boucher (t), HABS (l,a), LC, Farm Security Administration, Russell Lee (r,a).

2. *The Essentials: Windows, Doors, Ceilings, and Floors:* p. 24, LC-HABS, Jack E. Boucher (t and a); p. 25, LC-HABS, Jack E. Boucher (t), LC-HABS (b); p. 26, LC-HABS, Jack E. Boucher (t and m), HABS (b); p. 27, LC-HABS (t and a); p. 28, LC-HABS (b); p. 29, LC-HABS (t); p. 30, LC-HABS (m); p. 31, LC-HABS (t), HABS, Philip Turner (a).

3. *A Portfolio of Period Living Rooms and Parlors:* pp. 33-35, Eric Schweikardt; pp. 36-38, Bert Denker; pp. 39-44,

Allison Abraham; p. 45, Eugene Valenta; p. 46, Mark Gottlieb; pp. 47-54, Michael Kanouff; pp. 55-56, Mark Gottlieb;
pp. 57-60, Michael Kanouff; pp. 61-62, Mark Gottlieb; p. 63,
Michael Kanouff; p. 64, Eugene Valenta.

4. *The Architectural Elements: Millwork, Plasterwork, and
Hardware:*   p. 65, LC-HABS; p. 67, LC-HABS (t); p. 68, LC-
HABS (l,t); p. 70, HABS (m), LC-HABS (b); p. 71, LC-HABS
(l,t), LC-HABS, Gerda Peterech (r,t), LC-HABS, Ned Goode
(b).

5. *Paints, Papers, and Fabrics:*   p. 73, LC-HABS (t and a); p.
74, LC-HABS (l and r); p. 75, LC-HABS, Jack E. Boucher (l);
p. 76, LC-HABS (t), HABS, Laurence E. Tilley (b); p. 77, *A
Book of Studies in Plant Form and Design* (1902) by A. E. V.

Lilley and W. Midgley (b); p. 78, LC-HABS (t); p. 79, LC-
HABS (b); p. 80, LC-HABS; p. 82, LC-HABS, Cortlandt V.
D. Hubbard (r).

6. *Furnishing the Period Living Room and Parlor:*   p. 84, *The
Practical Book of Period Furniture* (1914) by Harold
Donaldson Eberlein and Abbot McClure (t and b); p. 85,
Period Furnishings (1914) by C. R. Clifford (t and m), LC-
HABS, Cortlandt V. D. Hubbard (b); p. 86, HABS (l,t), LC-
HABS (l,m), LC-HABS, Jack E. Boucher (r,b).

P. 90, LC-HABS, Jack E. Boucher; p. 91, LC-HABS, Ned
Goode; p. 92, HABS, Susan M. Dornbusch; p. 93, LC-HABS;
p. 95, LC-HABS.

Selected Bibliography

Only those publications currently in print are included in this listing.

Benjamin, Asher. *The American Builder's Companion.* New York: Dover Publications, reprint 1969.

Bicknell, A. J. *Victorian Village Builder.* Watkins Glen, N.Y.: The American Life Foundation & Study Institute, reprint 1976.

Bicknell, A. J. and W. T. Comstock. *Victorian Architecture.* Watkins Glen, N.Y.: The American Life Foundation & Study Institute, reprint 1978.

Brightman, Anna. "Window Treatments for Historic Houses, 1700-1850." Technical Leaflet No. 17. Washington, D. C.: National Trust for Historic Preservation, n.d.

Cummings, Abbott Lowell. *Bed Hangings: A Treatise on Fabrics and Styles in the Curtaining of Beds, 1650-1850.* Boston: The Society for the Preservation of New England Antiquities, 1961.

_____. *Rural Household Inventories Establishing the Names, Uses, and Furnishings of Rooms in the Colonial New England Home.* Boston: The Society for the Preservation of New England Antiquities, 1964.

Downing, A. J. *The Architecture of Country Houses.* New York: Dover Publications, reprint 1969.

Eastlake, Charles Locke. *Hints on Household Taste.* New York: Dover Publications, reprint 1969.

Frangiamore, Catherine Lynn. *Wallpapers in Historic Preservation.* National Park Service Publication No. 185, Technical Preservation Services Division. Washington, D.C.: Office of Archeology and Historic Preservation, 1977.

Handlin, David P. *The American Home, Architecture and Society, 1815-1915.* Boston: Little, Brown and Co., 1979.

Little, Nina Fletcher. "Historic Houses: An Approach to Furnishing." Technical Leaflet No. 17. Nashville, Tenn.: American Association for State and Local History, 1970.

Loth, Calder and Julius Trousdale Sadler, Jr. *The Only Proper Style, Gothic Architecture in America.* Boston: New York Graphic Society, 1975.

Nylander, Jane C. *Fabrics for Historic Buildings.* Washington, D.C.: The Preservation Press, 1977.

Page, Marian. *Historic Houses Restored and Preserved.* New York: Whitney Library of Design, 1976.

Peterson, Harold L. *American Interiors from Colonial Times to the Late Victorians.* New York: Charles Scribner's Sons, 1971.

Seale, William. *Recreating the Historic House Interior.* Nashville, Tenn.: American Association for State and Local History, 1979.

_____. *The Tasteful Interlude: American Interiors through the Camera's Eye.* New York: Dover Publications, 1975.

Vaux, Calvert. *Villas and Cottages.* New York: Dover Publications, reprint 1970.

Wharton, Edith and Ogden Codman, Jr. *The Decoration of Houses.* New York: W. W. Norton & Co., reprint 1978.

Whiffen, Marcus. *American Architecture Since 1780.* Cambridge, Mass.: The M.I.T. Press, 1969.

Index

Since the terms "Colonial" and "Victorian" are far too broad to be anything but generally descriptive, they do not appear in this index. Consult the breakdown of the larger periods into component parts (i.e., Georgian, Gothic Revival, Italian Villa) under Architectural styles.

People who live in and love old houses (or new houses in a traditional style) are constantly searching for ideas, products, and services to improve their homes.

In our effort to bring you the best possible information on old houses, we hope you will share your expertise with us. We would like to know what products or services you would recommend that we might consider for inclusion in the next edition of THE BRAND NEW OLD HOUSE CATALOGUE. And we hope you will let us know what titles would be helpful additions to our OLD HOUSE series.

Please send your recommendations to: Lawrence Grow, c/o Special Sales Department, Warner Books, 75 Rockefeller Plaza, New York, N.Y. 10019.

THE OLD HOUSE BOOKS
Edited by Lawrence Grow

THE BRAND NEW OLD HOUSE CATALOGUE
3,000 Completely New and Useful Products, Services, and Suppliers for Restoring, Decorating, and Furnishing the Period House—From Early American to 1930s Modern
#97-557   224 pages $9.95 in quality paperback; $17.95 in hardcover

THE OLD HOUSE BOOK OF BEDROOMS
96 pages, including 32 color pages
#97-553 $7.95 in quality paperback; $15.00 in hardcover

THE OLD HOUSE BOOK OF LIVING ROOMS AND PARLORS
96 pages, including 32 color pages
#97-552 $7.95 in quality paperback; $15.00 in hardcover

Forthcoming:
THE OLD HOUSE BOOK OF OUTDOOR LIVING SPACES
THE OLD HOUSE BOOK OF DINING ROOMS AND KITCHENS
THE OLD HOUSE BOOK OF HALLS AND STAIRCASES

Look for these books in your favorite bookstore. If you can't find them, you may order directly by sending your check or money order for the retail price of the book plus 50¢ per order and 50¢ per book to cover postage and handling to: Warner Books, P.O. Box 690, New York, N.Y. 10019. N.Y. State and California residents, please add sales tax.